FEARLESS
WOMAN

Overcoming Everything that was Meant to Destroy Me

Chana Brown

ISBN: 978-1-953760-00-5

Published by Pure Thoughts Publishing, LLC
2055 Gees Mill Rd #316 | Conyers, GA 30013 USA
470-440-0875 | www.purethoughtspublishing.com
Printed in the United States of America

TABLE OF CONTENTS

DEDICATION

I dedicate this book to my children. Believe in yourself and all that you are. Know that there is something inside you that is greater than any obstacles. I love you.

ACKNOWLEDGMENTS

I would like to express special thanks to my publisher, Dr Marita Kinney. Thank you for bringing my story to life.

INTRODUCTION

I appreciate you for taking the time to read my story. I want to encourage you all to never give up. There is always a new beginning from a dark place. I hope that my story can encourage many women and men out there who are going through this in their lives or has experienced something similar. I know I'm not the only one who has gone through this. I want to encourage you to find the strength in whatever you're going through, find the strength to overcome obstacles, fears, pain, and abuse .. never let your past define who you are. You are not your past.

CHAPTER ONE

When Everything Changed

My mom was 16 years old when she had me. We lived with my grandma. She would take me to the park and watch me play before taking me over to her friend's house. When I was about four years old, my mother moved into her own apartment. My dad would spend time with me and buy me nice things. I remember the day I was hospitalized, my mom and dad argued. Daddy was very upset because I got really sick. It was a normal day, me and Mom were at Grandma's house. At that time we were still living with Grandma before mom moved into her own apartment. Grandma had kerosene on the table, which I picked up and started drinking; I thought it was Kool-Aid. Shortly after that, I was rushed to Grady Hospital, where I was admitted. Dad came to the hospital upset, and he and Mom started arguing about what happened. I remember Dad asking Mom what the hell happened and then picking up a chair and throwing it at her.

Once my mom moved into her first apartment, I was so happy. She would always take me to the store and walk me to my grandma's house. She would sometimes let me go to my dad's mom's house, so I could visit her and play with my cousins and my aunt there. I would see them all the time, and they'd have gifts, clothes, and nice things for me. We would also have picnics outside on the porch. At times, I would see Mom and Daddy argue and fight.

When I was about five years old, my mom lived in the projects, in a one-bedroom apartment. She was a beautiful lady with a light complexion, medium build, standing about 5'2", with shoulder-length hair, and was physically fit with a pretty smile. She would always cook for me every day. She'd cook breakfast, lunch, and dinner for me. My mom would also get me dressed and made sure that I looked pretty. She would walk me to the store, to the park and watch me play. We'd always do the laundry together. My mom used to go out in the backyard and hang the clothes up, and I would help her. Every morning, my mom would get me dressed for school and walk me to school every day. Each morning we walked to school, she would to tell me, "Holly," it was short for Hollywood, "look both ways before you cross the street." Every afternoon, Mom would pick me up from school and every day, either she would have a snack for me or she was cooking on the stove.

We would return home and have our mother-daughter-time, where we would watch cartoons, and I'd play with my kitchen set. My mom would be in there with me. We would either be cooking on my kitchen set or playing with my dolls. My mom also taught me how to color. Every other weekend, we would catch the bus to Grandmama's house. We would stay for the weekend and come back. And my mom did the same thing every day: she got up, walked me to school, and then picked me up. And then I saw a man in my mom's home one day, and she introduced me to him, telling me that he was her friend. My Mom changed as time went by; she didn't cook anymore, and she didn't get me dressed like she normally would. My mom didn't take me to school anymore either.

I became independent, going through the refrigerator to see what I wanted to eat and getting up in the morning, trying to find my clothes to get myself dressed for school. I was late getting to school; I knew I was late because I hadn't seen the other parents walking their kids to school. I was alone. I was late because I had to start getting up on my own in the mornings. I walked to school from memory from when my mom used to take me. I started to feel sad and scared because I was walking through a pathway by myself to get to school. I knew how to cross the street because my mom taught me how to; she taught me how to look right and left, and how to watch out for the cars. When school ended, I was hoping that she'd be there to pick me up like old times, but I'd be disappointed and had to walk back home alone. My mom was barely helping me with my homework. We no longer went to the store. We no longer did the things that we used to do. She started leaving me at home by myself to go hang out. I was scared. One night, Mom left me alone in the house, and I remember walking to the window and screaming out the window so that someone could hear me. I was crying and scared because Mom left me alone.

I did this every day, hoping that one day, my mom would get up and go back to the way she was before she met that guy. The man began fighting and hitting my mom, and she'd cry. And her behavior kept changing. My mom would have a lot of company over; they were constantly in and out of our house. They would come over to do marijuana or drugs. The man moved in after that, and he started selling drugs from my mom's home.

One day he got rid of all of our stuff, and furnished the apartment very lavishly. I had never seen furniture like that before. We went to Grandma's house one day, and when we came back, all of the furniture that he had put in my mom's house was gone; the apartment was empty. He had sold it all. We had no sofa. We had no tables. There was only one bed, with only a mattress and a box spring. Me and my mom slept on the mattress; we didn't have anything anymore.

One day I came home from school, and my mom had pots on the stove, and she said, "Go wash your hands." I went to wash my hands, and the next thing I knew, I heard banging on the door. "Go upstairs, go upstairs," she said. But I never ran upstairs. It was the SWAT team raiding our home.. I can remember the dog sniffing around the laundry room where me and mom would do the laundry. The dog found bags of weed. They arrested my mom, and I can remember her crying and saying, "Call my mom. So my mom could come and get my baby." And I was crying, as I was scared. I didn't know what the police were going to do, if they were going to take me away, but I was quiet because I saw my mama going away. A couple of weeks later, my mom was released. And from that point on, we moved in with my grandma.

I was about five years old when witnessed all of that. Before my mom started to date that guy, ended up on drugs, and having a lot of friends over, our life was normal.

Chapter Two

The Safe Place

Shortly after we moved in with Grandma, I saw my mom less. I saw more of my grandma, who pretty much took over the responsibility of raising me. She enrolled me in school and made sure that I attended, that I had clothes, that I ate, and that I had everything I needed. When holidays came around, birthdays, etc., Grandmama never forgot about me.

My grandma moved around a lot. I was in and out of different schools. We moved to so many different places. My grandma was always there for me. I always expected affection, , for her to nurture me, be loving to me, be compassionate, and caring. Grandma would say, "I love you," but she never showed it. She just bought me things. "I know you need these things. And here," she would say. But I never got the hugs, the kisses, or affection. Grandma just took care of me.

My mom came around every so often. I saw her face sometimes, but not consistently. I never really had any contact with her; I never called her.

This one time, my mom came to my grandma's house and told me, "I'm going to take you to my friend's house." She took me to one of our old neighborhoods, where my grandmother once lived, and she took me to her friend's house where they were hanging out and getting high.

"Holly, you can play with her kids," she said.

I replied, "I'm staying here."

She told me again, "You go outside and play with the kids."

So all day, I played with the kids; we played and played, and it got later and later. But I never saw my mom again. I never saw her leave. I didn't know who came to get her. I sat on top of the hood of a white car and watched all the kids going into their houses because it was getting dark outside. I went to my mom's friend and asked, "Where's my mom?" It was during the winter, and it was getting extremely cold.

"I don't know where your mom is," she replied.

"You don't know where my mom is? Well, can I use the phone to call my dad?" I asked.

And she said, "Yes, baby, you can use the phone to call your dad."

I always kept my dad's number. I called my dad and my other grandma picked up the phone. She asked me if I was okay. I told her, "No." She asked me what was going on. I asked her, "Would you come and get me?" They came and picked me up from my mom's friend's house and they were very upset.

I heard them in the car saying, "This can't keep happening. She's unfit. We got to take her. We got to do something about this."

The police arrived shortly after, and I can remember the police telling me to get in the car, and my dad was fussing.

"Don't worry about it. We're going to work it out," they said. "We're going to try to take this to court to try to get custody of you. We want you to stay with us."

And at the time, I was saying yes because I was in a situation where I needed to be around my dad because my mom was not around and my grandma was not showing me love and affection, The police then drove off, and I can remember my dad saying, "Don't cry, I'm coming to get you baby. The police took me to a place where I had no idea where I was, and I saw a lot of beds. A lady told me I was at a shelter group home, and I can remember being sad and having dried up tears on my face from crying.

In my dad's household, it was stricter, with "yes ma'am, no sir." That's how I was taught to talk and how I was raised to speak to my grandparents.

The next couple of days we went to court where they tried to get custody. But the judge didn't give me over to my dad because my last name was different from his. I was not registered with my dad's last name; I was registered in another person's name. Mom was in court saying, "Don't give my daughter to him because that's not her dad. She's in somebody else's name."

I can remember my mama pulling out the birth certificate saying, "We don't want her with him. We feel he's not a good fit for my daughter." That's when I found out I was registered with another person's name who wasn't my biological father.

She said that I could stay with her mom. And shortly after that, I never went to anyone. I went right back to a shelter, and I stayed there for a month or so. I never knew why I was there. I just knew that the police took me there. A social worker was in the car when the police took me there and I didn't have any clothes. They told me to stay there.

They didn't give me any time as to how long I was going to stay . I was just in a place with strangers, scared and missing my grandma and my mom. I didn't know if Dad or my other grandparents were going to walk through the door or if they could get me out.

I was there for maybe two months. I wasn't in school. The other kids were going to school, but I was never registered. I was just there every day. I would get up out of bed, make the bed up in the mornings, and come out in the dayroom to watch TV, eat lunch, color, and all of that stuff. I used to go to a playground where they would take us to do activities. One day this white man came into my room. I was sitting on the bed. He said, "Chana, I got good news. Do you want some cookies?"

I replied, "Yes."

He said, "You're going to see your Auntie Cookie. You're going to her house."

I jumped up and said, "I'm going to my auntie's house!" At that time, I felt grateful because I was going to someone's house outside of the foster home and it was a family member. I was so excited to go to my aunt's house. As long as I got out, that was all that mattered. They got me ready, packed my things, and took me to my aunt's house. She and her husband welcomed in. They assigned me to my room and went over the house rules. However, I was a little confused when I got there because my grandma was staying there. I wondered why my grandmother didn't come to get me instead of my aunt.

Things were a little different because, although my grandmother lived there too, my aunt was mostly responsible for me. She would cook dinner. Every morning

I would go to the same school, but this time Grandma was taking me every single morning. She would drop me off and come back and pick me up each and every morning and afternoon. One particular day, Grandma never showed up at school to pick me up. I stood in front of the school and watched as the kids got on the school bus and car riders, getting in the car with their parents. I saw kids walking back through the pathway I used to walk when I lived across the street in the apartments. I remained where I was, and I think the school closed because everyone was gone. I started crying. I was cold and afraid. I felted scared, lonely, and abandoned. But I kept looking, hoping to see that white car. I never saw that car. I knew the way to get back because I paid attention to my grandma when she drove. I knew every neighborhood. After waiting a long time, I decided to walk home. I was eight years old, maybe seven. I just started walking in the direction that her car would have gone. After walking an hour or so, a red truck pulled up and the man inside said, "Hey baby are you ok? I have candy and a drink for you," he said and gave me a Coca Cola. As I began to drink it, he said asked me, "How did you get here, baby?" I told him I walked from school. At the time, I wasn't taught not to speak with strangers. All thought about was that I was extremely cold, and my hands were freezing; I nearly had frostbites on my fingers. I wanted heat. I was ready to get warm. So I got in the truck, and he said, "If I can take you home, do you mind telling me where you stay?"

I replied, "Sure." I was very smart. He took me all the way home. When we pulled up, I was so happy when I saw my house. *I'm home.*

"Be careful," he told me and then pulled off.

When I knocked on the door, my aunt answered. "What happened? How did you get here?" she asked.

Then Grandma came in and said, "Oh baby, I forgot to come to pick you up. It slipped my mind."

"Mom, how did you forgot to pick her up?" my aunt asked.

"I don't know. I had things going on. I had things I had to do. I was trying to do a million things and I forgot to pick her up," Grandma replied.

That's when my aunt said, "This can't happen again." My aunt later enrolled me in the school that her kids attended. I stayed with them for maybe a month or two until my grandmama moved and I left with her. But I would often spend weekends at my Aunt Cookie's house. I had the best time there ..

I always reminisced about when I was staying with my mom before she was on drugs. That thought always came to my mind. I wished I could be with my mom again. I never understood why she never came back for me. At that age, I didn't understand anything about the type of drugs and how they affected my mom, and how it caused her not to be around.

I always hoped and wished that my mom would one day show up. Whenever she did show up, I'd get really happy to see her and wouldn't act distant towards her. She'd stay briefly and would mostly sleep, then leave again. She didn't stay long at all, maybe three or four hours. I guess she was tired from staying up all night and running through the streets. She would come over just to rest and would not be bothered with me. She never asked me how school was, asked me if I was okay, gave me kisses, or anything. I never got that from my mother or my grandmother. My grandma would get up, go to work and then come back home. That was her normal routine.

I remember my grandmother asking my mother to get custody of me and my mom said, "No, you just want her for a check. You just want her for money."

My grandmother replied, "Well, I'm taking care of her. I think I should have custody of her."

"I'm not giving my rights up," my mom told her. My grandmother then went on to explain to her that she wasn't using the money to provide for me, that her lifestyle was unsafe, and that she couldn't take care of me. Although my mom had the money, she didn't have shelter or a car. My mom didn't have anything she had before the drugs.

My grandmother and I continued to move from place to place. I remember having anxiety problems due to missing my mother so much. My grandmother and mother told me that's what caused it. They said that I used to rock back and forth a lot. I'm not sure what caused it, but I was going through a lot mentally.

My grandmother tried her best though. I can remember having the best Christmases and birthdays ever. She made sure to bake me cakes for my birthday and around Christmas time. She would always wake me up and have all my toys and everything that I wanted or had asked for. My dad used to buy me gifts on the holidays too. He would come to get me on weekends, and we would go to the carnival, shopping, and to a friend's house. Dad would call me Boont and said I would always be his Boont. Those were some of my happiest memories from childhood because things weren't always bad.

CHAPTER THREE

The Turning Point Part 1

By this time, my grandma had moved to another location, and my aunt was living there with her daughter, who is my cousin, and we used to play outside, walk to the store and go to school. That's what the everyday routine was for me and my cousin. We both did the same things. Whatever she saw me do, she'd do it too. My grandmother still worked a lot, and when she left, my mom and aunt could have company over. They would cook all of my grandma's food, get high, and play music. They would tell me and my little cousin to go in the room or go outside, and we used to do what they say, staying out of grown folk's business. The guys that would come over to see them would sometimes give us $2 and tell us how pretty we were. This went on practically every Thursday and Friday, twice a week; it went on for a whole month. They just kept coming over. I'm sure that my grandmother didn't know about it.

One particular time when my grandmama went to work, they came over. I can remember two of the guys asking, "Do y'all want to go to the store? Let's go to the store to get you guys something."

And we said, "Okay." So we put on our shoes, walked down the steps, and got in the car. My mom knew that we were leaving. I noticed that we went past the store and we began looking at each other. As they passed it, "I said, well, where are we going?"

"Just hold tight. We're going to take you out. We're going to take you out to the store," he replied. At that point, we both were scared.

We didn't know where we were about to go, both our moms were at the house and we were in the car with strangers. As we rode, I began to hear airplanes. I can remember looking up at the sign that read, *Hartsville*. By then, we pulled up at the airport. When we pulled up to the airport, they told me to stay in the car and the dad got out with my cousin. He told her, "You're coming with me." I guess one man was the dad and the other was the son. "I'm about to go pick up another friend," the dad said. I was left alone with the other man.

The man was touching me and was asking me, "Have you ever had sex before?"

I told him, "No, I never done it before."

He said, "You and her stole my money."

"I don't steal money," I said.

He had his hand around my neck and was pushing on my chest. I was getting even more scared, and I started crying. I was alone with this grown man, and I was only 11 years old. Then I remember him getting in the driver's seat and he just started driving. He was driving fast and running red lights. I thought that we were going to crash. I was terrified; I was just a kid. After he drove around, he came back to the airport, and by then, the guy came out with my little cousin and another guy. The guy loaded his luggage in the trunk of the car. He got in the car with all of us and we drove off again. They said, "We got to stop by the store." I got left in the car again. The dad got out again with my cousin and the other man. They were in the store for maybe 10 to 15 minutes. While they were inside of the store, the guy/son got back in the driver's seat and again began to do the same things to scare me, driving fast and asking for his money. We came back and my cousin came out of the store looking scared too. She got back into the car, and we both were thinking, *We've got to go home.* The man who they picked up from the airport, we went to his apartment, and they said, "Get out the car right now." We were scared to get out of the car. I recall going into this apartment and seeing a lot of water on the carpet. "We need you guys to stand right here and pull your clothes down because we know y'all stole our money," they said.

"We didn't take any money," we replied and just cried and cried and cried. We were crying so hard. We didn't know what they were going to do. Maybe torture us. We just knew that we weren't safe. We got back in the car and the man that they picked up stayed at his apartment.

On the way home, they said, "Y'all better not say something. If you say anything, you're going to hear from us again."

We agreed not to say anything. And by the time we got home, our grandmama was off of work. "Where y'all been at?" she asked.

"Grandma, we went to the store," we answered. We had no snacks, nothing in our hands.

She said, "If y'all went to the store, what did y'all get?"

"We ate it coming back," we lied. But my mom and auntie knew what they had done. They knew they had sent us off. They were covering up the night. They didn't want Grandma to know. Me and my cousin, lived with that secret for a while. We never saw those men again, and we eventually told Grandma what happened.

Right after that, Grandma moved again to the apartments across the street. It was a neighborhood full of drug dealers, drug addicts; it was pretty much the ghetto.

I witnessed so much crime, violence, the older men chasing after the young girls. I was scared for a while to go outside. I eventually started to leave the apartment and began to meet different people. I met different friends, started hanging out, and was just having a good time. My mom still came around from time to time. She would sometimes chastise me and ask why did I do something that she had heard about and tried to whoop me. My aunt used to tell her, "You're not in her life. You just can't come in and out and just do that to her." My mom was heavily on drugs by this time and she would get upset if she couldn't get high. If I was anywhere around, she'd try to hit me. I had to go through all of that. I was being abused physically by a lot of people. I got abused by two uncles. I was also abused by my Mom verbally. I went through the worst in my life at this time.

At this point, I was truly suffering. I was going to school, telling the school that everybody in the house was on drugs, and asked if they could come and save me, please. I went to the counselor and the school came out for a home visit. My grandma and my mom told them that I was crazy and not to believe me. They told the school that everything was going well at home. I began to just sweep everything under the rug and they did too.

My uncle was very abusive. I watched him fight my mom and my aunties, and he'd beat us. One day he was fighting my mom because everybody that lived there was on drugs, and I jumped in, and hit him. He hit me so hard, I can remember seeing stars. My whole face was swollen, turning black. When I went to school, the teacher asked, "How did you get blood clots?" I knew that I had to lie. She asked, "Did someone do this to you?" I told her that I got hit in the eye with the keys. I did what my grandmama told me to do.

When my uncle did that. I called the police that night and told the police his name. I remember my grandmother taking up for him by saying, "That's not his name. She doesn't know what she talking about." My grandma always swept things under the rug, and I just wanted a way out. I didn't feel any compassion at home. I was in a dysfunctional and broken home. I was tortured while living in a house with addicts. I felt like the black sheep and I was always getting beat up. I was tired of being hit and cussed out.

My dad had a heart, and at times he would get upset and would verbally abuse me too. I always wanted that fatherly love from him but felt disconnected. My feelings were so hurt because of the pain that it caused me. We became distant and would see each other from time to time as the years went by. We would never stay on good terms. He would drink often and get upset. I never understood why my dad treated me this way. All I wanted was for him to be proud of me and acknowledge me and my efforts. Sometimes I felt as though I didn't have a dad. I remember he treated me kind in my early childhood.

My life continued to change. Me and my oldest cousin always did each other's hair and got dressed to catch the bus to the mall. We would have late-night conversations and sometimes we would fight then makeup. We'd sometimes sneak out of the house to go to house parties and skipped school to hang out with friends. We were more like sisters growing up, and our Grandma would fix good ole Sunday dinners.

Later on, I met this young guy named D. I met him in the neighborhood; we started talking and it soon became a relationship. I'd tell him what I was going through in the house. And I'd always ask him, "Do you love me? Can you love me?" And he'd always tell me he loved me too. I fell in love with this guy and I thought we were meant for each other. We started courting and hanging out often. I became sexually active, losing my virginity at the age of 12. Shortly after, we started running away together to be with each other every chance we got. I would skip school and run away from home to be with him.

I stayed in abandoned apartments or at our neighbor's house, and we had sex often. We would tell each other that we love each other all the time. He told me he felt like the black sheep and that he always wanted to run away. We ran away constantly for about two months. Every time I had money, I'd catch the bus to meet him, and we'd run away together. We felt all we had was each other and we were tired of being abused or mistreated at home. We would sleep over at his uncle's house sometimes. I would do anything to escape my house. My grandma was moving everybody in whenever they'd lose their place. Grandma's house was everyone's safety net when they fell on hard times. So our house was crowded and everyone there was on drugs and very abusive to me. So that's what made me run away consistently.

At school, I fought with kids every day. I lashed out because I had so much anger and stress inside of me. I wanted to fight and beat up somebody every single day. I would just walk up to people and fight them; I was bitter. The teachers used to ask me, "What's going on?" I never really told the teachers everything that was going on in my home. I was bitter. I was angry. I had become an angry child.

As time went by, and as I continued to run away, I eventually got pregnant at 13 years old. I was scared and afraid of my father finding out. I was scared to become a teen mom. My mom wasn't surprised. I told my grandma, and she called my dad. He came over and sat me down to talk. He asked," What are we going to do about this?"

"I don't know," I replied.

He was disappointed but took me to the doctor, I had two or three visits. He didn't want me to go through with the pregnancy. "You're not going to have no kids. You're just 13 years old," he told me. So, we tried to go have an abortion, but the nurse told my dad that I was too far along. So he said, "Well, .what? You're just going to have to have the baby." At that moment I was so scared. I realized that I was going to have a baby.

As I got bigger during my trimester, parents stopped allowing their kids to come around. Teachers were whispering and talking about me in school and talking to me in any kind of way. I wasn't even sitting seven months and they stopped me from going to school. I guess I was becoming a distraction. . All of my cousins that lived at my grandma's house were in school. Everybody was going to school except for me. I was that young, sitting at home every day, walking around the apartment, pregnant. I didn't know what to do. I'll never forget my mom told me, "Oh, you pregnant, you going to have a house full of children." I wasn't expecting that. I'm not sure what I expected, but it wasn't that.

Ideally, I wanted my family to embrace me and to be supportive. But I knew that wasn't going to happen. My mom was too far gone on drugs and didn't care. She never asked me what I was having. Are you okay? Are you going to the doctor? None of that. My dad took me to every doctor's appointment. My daddy was there through the whole nine months from the beginning to the end.

Grandma continued to make sure that I had a place to stay. My grandma would cash my mom's check and give me all the money because she knew I was a child having a child and that I would need the money. She would say, "You take this money. I don't want anything out of it. And you just buy for you and the baby."

She did that every month because my momma was never there to get the checks. So, my grandma would sign a check for her and cash it, and she would just give me the money. I had to grow up so fast; I missed out on my childhood. I went from a teenager to a mother.

Before I became a teen mom, I would hang out with my friends every day, we would, walk around the neighborhood, meet up to go to the mall, carnival, dance, and take the bus downtown. I enjoyed those times ... My best friend Nicole understood me and I understood her. I would often go to her house to have dinner and we would laugh and joke around, watch movies, and just hang out. She was my BEST FRIEND .. we became long-time friends.

During the time when I was pregnant, I'd go to my neighbor's house because so much was going on in my home. I mentioned all that was going on before I got pregnant, just imagine all that at the time of my pregnancy. I wanted to protect my baby from all of that chaos. I didn't want my baby to get abused or to get hit while I was pregnant. I realized that I had a person growing inside of me who was depending on me. I would always talk to my stomach, saying, "What? I don't care if you're a boy or girl, I love you." I would think to myself, *My family don't love me.*

Maybe this baby will love me. No one else had truly loved me. I felt that way because they weren't showing me love.

It seemed. everybody was against me; my family would always comment on me being 14 and pregnant; everybody would bash me. It hurt so bad. I was getting backlash from everybody, even my family. I had a lot of stress. I was also going through it with the father of the child. We were going back and forth due to me being pregnant and my hormones made me extremely moody. Things began to go downhill with us for a while.

I'll never forget the day that I went into labor; it was on Valentine's day. I was hurting so bad. I had wanted to go out to the mall, so I got dressed up. As I was getting dressed, I started to feel pain. I never felt pain like that before. It was a pain that I couldn't bear. I went on my knees and I started crying, but no one knew I was crying. I was feeling the pain from everything that was going on in my life. I was hearing the voices of the parents of my peers: "You can't be around her." The pain continued. I thought, *Maybe the baby is just moving around.* But then I felt it again and again. I finally went and told my grandma, I said, "I'm hurting." She asked me if I was in labor. I said, "I'm not sure."

She then said, "Okay, well, baby, just walk around." She called my dad over. We were walking around all throughout that day. We came back into the house and hours later I complained about the pain again.

Eventually, Grandma said, "We're not going to call the ambulance. I'm just going to take you down there. She went to looked for my mom first, but she was nowhere to be found. She kept looking and she eventually found her.

When my mom came into the house, she said, "You're really about to have the baby?" I was kind of happy to see my mom. I thought about her not being there in my life now that I was having a baby. We arrived at the hospital, and they admitted me. My mom, my dad, my grandma, and my aunt were all there to support me while I was in labor.

I can remember seeing my mom in the labor and delivery room with me, but she was falling asleep, and my dad was asking her to wake up. After 22 hours of pain, I remember the nurses saying, "We got to get this baby out. As soon as possible." I remember being on the bed and being rolled down the hallway. I saw lights and remember going into the operating room. I was so scared. They put monitors on me and a mask on my face. I felt traumatized. I thought, *What's going on*. I remember them taking my baby out. I never knew my baby's gender until they took the baby out and said, "It's a baby boy. The first time I saw my baby, I started crying.

Can I hold my baby?" I asked.

They replied, "Wait a minute."

I remember asking why I had to wait. They were cleaning my baby off and then handed him to me. I looked at my son and said, "I'm going to love you and I'm going to be here for you." I told him everything that I wanted to hear but never heard.

While in the hospital, I realized that I was a mother and a child. I was in disbelief. I was trying to comprehend everything. I knew that I was still a child, only 14 years old, and I didn't know what was next for me. A lot was going through my mind. I was having visitors and was still in disbelieve.

When I was discharged from the hospital, my motherly instinct kicked in right away. Once I got back home, I had no help or support from anyone. I had to get up every two hours, I had to change Pampers, I had to do everything alone. I had to make WIC appointments and become responsible right away because I had no one to teach me how to become a mom. My mom never showed me how. So, I didn't know. I just learned on my own; even before my child was born, I was on my own. No guidance, no one taught me anything. No one ever told me what was wrong and right, or you should do this and shouldn't do that. I had never experienced true guidance, only pain and abuse.

This part of my life was a turning point. After I had my son, I never went outside with my baby because we lived in the hood where you heard gunshots regularly. I didn't want to risk me, or my baby being shot, or being around a fight, or seeing drugs. Before I was pregnant, I used to be one of the girls out there fighting. Sometimes I'd see my mom walking through the apartment, going to the drug dealers, getting her drugs. My uncles would run in our house, asking my grandma to pay the drug dealers off because they owed someone money. I saw them do that a few times. Things were very hectic, but that was our life back then. It was no longer just me, I had a baby to protect too.

The Turning Point Part 2

I really had to step up as I went into motherhood. I had my son when I was in seventh grade. I went to junior high for a short period of time because I had no one to keep my son. I wanted to go to school so badly, but I couldn't. I used to offer my uncle, who stayed with us, money if he could watch the baby for me so I could go to school. I asked him to keep my baby for two days in the week. But no one helped. I had to stay home and watch kids get off of school, hoping that I could be the one to get off the bus one day. I always loved school.

Shortly after I went to my six-week postpartum checkup, I found out that I was pregnant with my second child. I was now 15 years old, and no one knew. My dad found out when I was five months and he said, "What are you going to do with that baby?"

"I'm not getting rid of that baby," I replied.

"Why not?" he had asked.

I told him, "I can feel my baby moving. And I'm not going to get rid of my baby."

He said, "You told me you weren't going to have no more kids."

I had found out that it was *a girl*, and so, I said, "Now I have my girl and my boy,", "my kids are going to love me, and I'm going to love my kids." That's all that I was thinking about.

My grandma moved again, and shortly after that, I gave birth to my second child. My aunt was staying there too, and we always fought, especially when Grandma was gone. My grandma worked at nights or the midnight shifts. I had gotten so tired of my aunt and I fighting. I'd go on the road with my two babies in my arms to try to keep them safe. I didn't want my kids to ever go through what I went through. I didn't want them to be abused and to mistreated. And because of the things that I went through, you know, I didn't want them to have parents like mine. ., there are just these . ideas. So at that time, when I went on and My grandmama told me, "I'm back to move again. And I want you to go stay with your aunt."

I replied, "I don't want to stay there."

She said, "You got to."

We were in junior high and still in a relationship when we had our second child. I was 16 years old, and I was still staying with my grandma, but I knew that I would end up moving. I found out that my kids' dad was arrested for murder. He went to jail, and I didn't know when he was going to be released. With him gone, I felt all alone with just my kids. I felt like my boyfriend was the only person who loved me. I was in love. We had been together since we were 12 years old. We were 16 now. So I was crying; I was left with two kids. *What I'm going to do?* I thought. Because at the time that we had the kids, even though we were young, I didn't know how he was getting the money to take care of them, but he would provide for them. It wasn't a lot, but he did it. He was buying diapers, milk, and things of that nature, clothes and shoes too, but he went to jail. He'd be gone for two years. Some weekends I would go to Club Sharon Showcase to hang out with friends, the only time I felt like a teenager again because I spent the majority of my time with my two kids, being a mom. The time came when Grandmama told me that she was about to move again, but I had to move with my auntie. I was upset because she knew that we didn't get along. So I moved in with my dad but things didn't work out and I was back at Grandma's house .

Later I moved in with my auntie and she ran the house. I paid her rent and bought food. There were a lot of people coming through her house, she had a lot of traffic. She stayed with a lot of company. They were getting high off drugs so I stayed upstairs with my kids to keep them out of the way of her company because that's how my auntie did. We continued to fight often, that's all I did staying with my aunt. She would get mad over something and kick me out.

This happened multiple times. She'd say, "You got to get out." I don't know what she was going through, but that's how I was being treated. My mom would come over every now and then. One day her guy friend had come over to pick her up. I was sitting on the couch and my mom was upstairs; her boyfriend touched me in an inappropriate way. I lived with that my entire life. My mom never did anything about it or said anything to him. I felt some type of way. Because I couldn't stay with my grandma... I thought, *Maybe my grandma got tired of me*. Maybe she thought, I done raise her. She got some kids. I can't raise no more. I'd wonder, *Why did my mom get rid of me? Why I'm here? Why did I come here?* I didn't get along with my aunt. I wanted to be back with my grandma. I'd always call her and asked to come back, but she would say, "It's just going to be me and your cousin, just us two. It just going to be me and her staying here. I raised you, you have kids now, you should stay with your aunt, that's better place for you." But it wasn't a better place because I was in the projects with more drugs and fighting. I was trying to protect my kids because there was so much going on. I was back in the same place that I started when she moved and when I got pregnant. From that point, my aunt just kept doing the same thing, telling me to get out. I was being verbally abused again by her. My kids' dad's mom took me in and I stayed with her a few months until things were a little better and I felt safer at home.

Once a month, I would visit my kids' dad, with his mom and the kids. Sometimes I would call her my mom because she was doing the things that my mom didn't do. Even though she didn't show me love by hugging and nurturing me, she did show me that she loved me and cared for me. She accepted me and my kids and went right into mom mode, She taught me how to really take care of my kids. I knew how to take care of kids, but she guided me in certain things and took me to get my first job. She taught me how to be independent, how to make my money. I worked for a while, but it wasn't mandatory that I work, I just wanted to get out and work because I felt that it was my responsibility to take care of my kids while their dad was in jail.

While my kids' dad was in jail for two years, I met this older guy; I was about 17 years old. He was 29 years of age. And at the time, I just felt lonely. When my son was admitted in the hospital, he came to visit with roses. He said, "I heard that your son got hurt. So I just came here to show you that I care."

"Okay, well, thank you," I replied. My auntie didn't live too far from the hospital. So he said, "I can pay for the taxi, or do you want to walk back?"

"Well, it's not late. We can all just walk back," I suggested. From that point, we started dating and ended up in a full-blown relationship. He became controlling, wanting to tell me what to do. He began talking to me very aggressively and became really violent. I found out that he was doing drugs. I thought, *Okay, that's why he was like that.* I felt like I was grown up now, as I was 17 and he was 29. This guy looked good too.

"I think you should move out," he stated one day

"Move out?" I questioned.

He said, "Yeah, we can get our own place."

So I ran it by my aunt. Her response was, "We might not get along, but I don't think you should leave."

"I want to leave because I want to be in my own place," I told her. I believed because I was older, at almost 18 and I had kids, I should be on my own. Against my better judgment, I moved out although my grandma told me not to do it. We moved into an apartment, but we didn't live there that long. We moved into another apartment and that's when the abuse became worse.

Whenever he got mad, he would pull guns on me or fight me. He'd abuse me a lot then come back and try to bribe me, telling me that he was sorry. I dealt with it because I was trying to stay away from my auntie's house. I just accepted it. Every time he mistreated me, he would go and get flowers, shoes, or he would give me money. He was verbally abusive, he'd hit me, lock me in the house and taking the keys so that I couldn't get out. I'd be stuck in this house all day. Cellphones weren't popular back then, so I couldn't call anybody. The only way I could call someone was if I went to a payphone.

I endured two months of that abuse. He had held me hostage. One particular day, he went to work and didn't lock the door. I told my kids, "Stay here." And they obeyed. When I walked to a payphone, I told my auntie about everything.

She said, "I told you to stay. Come back now."

I packed up all my and the kids' clothes. She sent me a taxi and I went back to her house. I figured he was going to come back for me. I was scared. I always locked the door. I felt that he'd eventually find me. I became scared and paranoid. "He's calling for you, what do you want me to say?" my grandma would tell me.

I said, "Don't say I'm here."

"I'm not going to tell him," she'd say. She then told me that he called for a week and threatened me.

The day before Christmas, I was lying in bed, and my kids were asleep. Suddenly, I heard my aunt screaming. I didn't hear the screaming for a while, then it began again. I said, "What's going on?" When I went to open up my door, he was running up the steps. I could see two bricks in his hands. I didn't know what to do. I knew he was going to kill me or hurt my kids. He hit me in my head and my face with the brick. At that point, I blanked out. I thought that I was dead. Somehow, I fought my way out of it, ran into my room, locked the door, and pushed the dresser behind it.

I can remember him saying, "When I come back B**tch, I'm going to kill you." Thankfully, he never came back.

I became a little bit antsy when my kids' dad was about to get out. When he was released from jail we eventually got back together.

I enrolled in school to get my GED and things were still going well. Everything was the same with my aunt, and then I got pregnant with my third child, all by the same guy.

During that time, my grandma took me to go look for an apartment. She said, "It's just not working out. So we're going to start trying to take you to look for your own apartment so you can have your own place."

And I said, "Okay."

"We're going to take you to apply for section eight housing," she told me. I didn't know what that was. She also put me on food stamps and Medicaid. She put me on everything from the government. So, she taught me how to do that. I remember her telling me, "You need this to help you out with your kids."

Until my section 8 came through, I ended up staying with my dad for a short period of time, and I had to endure verbal abuse from him. The verbal and physical abuse went on for a long period of time, on and off throughout my teenager, young adult life. Just imagine someone whom you thought loved you telling you I HATE YOU often.

Of course it didn't work out. So, after leaving there, my apartment came through; I got accepted. I moved into my first apartment. And there, I gave birth to my third child.

CHAPTER FOUR

Nowhere To Turn

Eventually, I moved into my second place, and I had three kids. While on section 8, I was about 20 years old and was still in a relationship with my kids' dad. He came by every so often. Sometimes he'd come by and sometimes he wouldn't. The relationship was on and off. He'd come and get the kids, or he would come and bring me money. He would help me out with the bills, food, or just about anything. That ended when he ended up going back to jail. He had another sentence, again.

I was left alone with three kids once again. I wasn't working at the time, I was just surviving and living with a welfare check and food stamps with zero rent. I was trying to make ends meet with a $330 welfare check and $200 worth of food stamps. I'd do my daily routine with the kids: cooking, making sure their homework was done, and walking my two oldest kids to school and to the park.

One day when the kids were at school, I decided to walk to the store by myself. When I walked into the store, this car came by and blew the horn. I was not paying any attention to the car, but the car pulled up beside me and the guy inside said, "You're a good-looking lady. Can I get your number?"

He looked like a dope boy. I could tell from the rim and his car. I used to be fascinated with that kind of stuff back then. I eventually took his number. "Call me when you get to the house," he told me. We started talking over the phone and he started to come over. Soon after, we started to get serious. When things started to get serious with us, he moved in with me. I thought things would be easier for me because it was a struggle only having little checks from the government and the kids' dad being gone. There was no money coming in and I wasn't going to call and ask family members for anything. At times, my lights would get cut off and I'd still try my best to manage with what I had.

I remember the guy coming over and asking, "Why is your house dark?" I was ashamed, but I told him that I didn't pay my electricity and they turned my lights off. He moved his things in. When he moved in, the lights were still off. We stayed in the apartment with no electricity for a month. I was wishing for somebody to could help me. Mom was staying with her friends and I told her about my situation. Life was really sad for me. It was cold and I couldn't make my kids the proper meal that they used to eat. The guy who my mom was dating actually paid to get the lights back on.

I became pregnant for the new guy. I was carrying my fourth child: my daughter. The guy stayed with me the whole time. When he moved in with me, he started meeting people in the area. He started going around different neighborhoods and houses, meeting and interacting with people I told him I didn't talk to a lot of people, but he became involved with them and got into an altercation with someone, and it got back to somebody else. This guy came looking for him. He knocked on the doors, but there was no answer, so he later came back and kicked in the door. I called my boyfriend's name. I told him to come down. I remember him having a gun in his hand. I remember asking what was going on? I think it was a drug deal gone bad.

They were going back and forth until things got really heated. The guy threatened to shoot up my house. So, I called my grandma and asked my grandma if I could come over until things settled down. And she said, "Yes, you come on over." I stayed at my grandmama's house for five days. I kept calling my boyfriend and asking him, what was going on. He told me that everything was okay. He stayed in the apartment to watch it while I was at my grandma's house with the kids. He left the key under the mat when he left. I told my grandma, "Okay, I feel better now," and thanked her and me and the kids went home. She told me that we could stay longer, but we left..

I wasn't there for not even five days, and I'll never forget what happened next. It was around one or two o'clock in the morning. All my kids were in the bed with me, and I heard loud gunshots. All I could think to do was to lay on my kids to make sure that they were ok. After the shots were fired, I walked down the steps and could see little bullet holes. I could see lights coming from the outside. I knew someone had shot through my door and I knew who they were shooting at.

I got so scared. I said, "Oh my God, someone's trying to kill me and my kids." I ran back upstairs and I took my dresser and put it behind the door. I just grabbed my kids. I was hoping and praying that the guy didn't kick the door completely in and come up there to kill me and my children. I heard another round of gunshots. Thankfully, we didn't get shot or hurt. We didn't get grazed by any bullets. I just heard the gunshots. They sounded like firecrackers. They were just coming back-to-back. I finally reached the phone in panic. The police came and they did a police report and took my statement.

That night, I left and never returned. I was terminated from section 8 housing. The property management put my things outside. I never tried to get it, I was too afraid. I moved back in with Grandmama. I went to her house with the three kids, still pregnant with the fourth baby on the way.

I stayed with Grandma until I was nine months pregnant. The entire time that I was staying there, she told me that I had to do something. That I couldn't come there with all the kids. "You're on your fourth baby. You got to do something. That was your responsibility for your company that you keep at your house," she said. By this time, my older children's dad was released from jail.

While I was in the hospital, in recovery after giving birth, I looked up from the bed and saw my cousin come into the room with my three kids. The doctor was looking like, *She just had a baby. She can't get up and move around, why are the kids here?* Thinking about the things that they used to do to me still sometimes hurts. They'd say, "We're not keeping no kids." And they brought my kids to me. I was sad and had just given birth. *I don't have nobody,* I thought *I have kids now with me and now a fourth baby, her dad was very supportive.*

All of my kids were there with me in the hospital room, I called my grandma to plead with her to make some arrangements for someone to come and get all my kids because I was still laying in a hospital bed. My grandma called me and said, "You got to find you a place to stay because you can't come here with that baby. I did all I could."

"Where am I going to go? I have nowhere to go," I pleaded.

"I don't know where you're going to go," she replied.

I made arrangements. I told my daughter's dad what was going on and asked if he could take care of the baby, and I'd find someone to watch my oldest children. That was the only idea that I came up with: to give my newborn to her dad, for her dad to take care of her because I had nowhere for me and my kids to go after my grandma said, "You can't come back here."

When I was released from the hospital, my newborn daughter went to her dad's house. I would go over to help out with her. He had her from birth until she was three months old. The other kids went with their grandma, their dad's mother. I was trying to keep the kids out of the street because I had nowhere to go.

When the baby got older and I got the older kids from their dad, I started going to shelters. I was going from shelter to shelter. I got kicked out of every shelter because my son was acting up. I think that he was acting up because we were in strange places. We had to get up every morning, three or four o'clock in the morning, just to get dressed. We'd leave and return in the afternoon. We had to deal with a lot of strangers. I didn't want to stay in a shelter, but I needed help and didn't want to be out in the cold with my kids. I would still keep a smile on my kids' faces; we would go out for lunch and ice cream and shopping. No matter what we were going through, I wanted my kids to feel happy during these hard times. I remember one late night riding the Marta trains and buses with my kids because we didn't have anywhere to go.

That situation went on for a while: bouncing around from shelter to shelter. Eventually, I thought, Okay, I can't do this. I got to figure something out. I don't know what I'm going to do, but I got to get my kids out the streets and I can't have them living with nobody. At times, my daughter's dad would take money from me, he would say he needed the money to Re-Up or whatever that meant, basically buying drugs to sell. I felt helpless because I was homeless at the time. I had nowhere to turn. I was trying to figure it all out. So, I decided to get a hotel room for me and my kids. I was tired of living in shelters. I wanted them to sleep comfortably and to be in a warm place. I didn't want them to be around strange people anymore.

After five days of being at the hotel, the man at the front desk told me that my time was up and that I couldn't have company there. I paid for five days, and I hadn't used all of my time. He said, "Someone, told me that you have been having company."

I told the man at the front desk, "I don't have company. I don't know who could have told you that. But me and my kids don't have anywhere to stay." I wanted to stay for the time that I had paid for. Regardless of what I said, he told me that I had to leave.

I began packing my things. We didn't have anywhere to go. We were sitting on the steps at the time, my baby was crying because she ran out of formula and the other kids were hungry. *I got to figure this out. What can I do to figure this out?* I thought. Child Protective Services kept playing in my head. And I kept saying, *No, I thought about that months ago, I can't do this to my kids.* I said to myself, *But if I do this, it's going to work out because my kids will no longer be in the streets, I can walk these streets, but not these kids.*

I had my last $40. I saw a man pass by, and I said, "Sir, could you come here for one second?"

"Sure," he replied.

"This is my last $40 and they put me out my room. Can you put the room in your name until tomorrow? I have a plan of how I am going to pay for it next week," I told him.

He said, "Sure, I'll do it." He left and never came back.

I was out in the cold with the kids, irritated. This guy said, "You can come in here and make some phone calls to someone who can come and pick you and your kids up."

I said, "Okay." So I went into the man's room.

We were staying in there, trying not to rush. We were looking at the TV and he asked my kids, "You hungry?" and gave them something to eat. Shortly after that, he said, "Have you made some type of arrangements? Because it's getting late."

I didn't know what to do. I had ran out of options. The only thing I knew to do was to call DFAC and put my kids in the system. This was like my third attempt; I had no other option. I picked up the phone and then I hung it up. I said, "I can't do this. Figure it out." I thought, *How are you going to figure this out? The kids are crying. They're getting irritated. They said that they want to lay down. They want to go to sleep.* I didn't know what to tell them.

I picked up the phone again. I called 911 and I told them what was going on. The man couldn't hear me talking and didn't know that I called 911. When they pulled up, I looked out the window and got all my kids and their bags and my clothes that I had. I walked to the lobby, and when the police came, he asked, "What's the problem?" I explained to the police I lost my place I had nowhere to go. I would come back for them. My oldest daughter, she was crying because she knew what was going to happen. My oldest son ran. He ran out of the lobby and hid in the kitchen. The third child, she was two. At the time, she was crying, wondering why everyone was crying and upset. The baby was screaming because she had no milk. I was feeding her soda and water. I didn't know what to do. I couldn't run and catch my son, and my oldest daughter was crying and complaining about her hand hurting. It was so much going on at that time. I was crying too. The police finally got the kids and put them in the police car. The police officer said, "Are you sure that you want to do this?"

I replied, "I'm sure."

My son was screaming, "Don't leave me!" He was screaming and kicking on the seats, yelling, "Mom, why are you leaving me?" I didn't have an answer for any of my kids.

I soon arrived at the hospital with my daughter. They took her right into surgery. They were saying something about her fingers. The surgery took about two hours. I called her dad, and he came down to see her. We were not in a relationship at this time. He asked me what was going on and what happened, but I never told anybody what I had done. I stayed there through her surgery and made every visit. During that time, I was also visiting my other children in DFAC. I had already begun going to court hearings. I left the hospital to attend a court hearing then went back to the hospital to see my daughter. I was aware that once she was discharged from the hospital that she would be going to a foster home.

CHAPTER FIVE

Finding My Way

In order to get the kids back, I had to complete different programs such as parenting classes and things like that. They wanted me to have a place to stay and a job. So, during that time, I was assigned to a caseworker and the caseworker would come over and give me different things to complete in order to get my kids back. They were just showing me what I needed to do get my kids back with me. They told me that I had to be stable in my job, have a place to stay, and had me apply for section eight again. I explained to them that I lost my section eight prior to that. But they still gave me the application to complete. I continued to do everything that they insisted that I do. I attended classes and different programs; it didn't matter. I was willing to do everything to have my kids back with me. I had to get everything done within two years because in two years, they could be adopted. At that time, I was pregnant again. One day I started to have bad cramps and pain, so I called the paramedics to the hospital and later to find out I had a miscarriage. I cried because of all the pain I endured. I felt so sad…

So at that time, I couldn't hold down a stable job. I was just bouncing around from job to job, but the section eight was approved. I was given the opportunity once again, and I found a place to stay. It was a four bedroom home and the kids would come over every weekend. I would have the kids on holidays, spring break, and their birthdays. All my kids would come over. I was able to go to the different schools where my two oldest attended. I'd sit with them, eat lunch with them, and things like that. My kids were in the system for 18 months. After a year and a half, we went back to court and they released my kids; they gave me back my kids, and I was so happy to have them back with me. Things were going well, but at times, I would run into hard times.

Once the kids came home, two years later, I was pregnant with the fifth child and last child. I was working a job that was paying me $10 an hour and had five kids on welfare. I was trying to make ends meet with my salary, a welfare check every month, and food stamps.

Raising kids alone, I didn't know where the next dollar would come from. I was running out of options. Raising five kids at 25 years old, I had to figure things out. How would I make it? I wasn't receiving child support. Grandma would help out and their dads would take them at times for weekends or just to spend time with them. My dad moved in to help out with the baby and the kids; he was a big help he helped around the house.

I decided to enroll in medical school. I graduated with high honors as a certified registered medical assistant, and I worked in the medical field for a few years. I chose to go to medical school because I always wanted to be a nurse as a little girl.

I could raise and take care of my kids the best way I could, making sure they were good. It made me happy to know that my kids were being taken care of. As A single mother working a minimum wage job, I did my best. I made sure my kids was safe, provided for them, and took them out to events. Things were still going okay; it could have been better. My daughter was later hospitalized and diagnosed with a brain tumor. Every man I met left me with another obstacle to overcome, feeling hurt, misled, or broken.

CHAPTER SIX

Survival

At this point in my life, no one was there to help me, I was trying to figure everything out. The kids' fathers were not helping me with the kids or in the children's lives consistently. I had very little income coming in. I was trying to make ends meet and every penny and dime was accounted for.

Sometimes I felt there wasn't any way out. It seemed as though something always came up and the kids were in need of something. My car was repoed so I was in survival mode. I was trying to keep the bill payments going and supporting five kids.

I was trying my best to provide for them. While I was going through this, my daughter started to run away, sometimes for a month or two; she was 14 years old. She would run away in the middle of the survival period; she wasn't going to school. I would ride around after work looking for her. I was trying to work, and my daughter was out in the streets.

When my daughter turned 15, I found out that she was pregnant with her first child. I was really hurt and angry. I felt ashamed and sad. I felt the pressure of another child that I'd have to take care of. I wasn't ready to be a grandma, I was still trying to make ends meet with my own children, trying to make sure my kids had what they needed. I was responsible for taking care of everybody. My daughter was young, so it was just me having to take care of another child. I didn't know what to do. My youngest daughter's father was sentenced to 15 years in prison, and I was left with another fatherless child to take care of alone. As time went by, my daughter finally gave birth to my grandson. I was mentally prepared to take care of another baby by myself.

My son started getting into trouble with the law, he ended up getting a burglar charge and was locked up. I was so stressed out. My son was gone and I was hurt about it because my son was going away at 17 years old. With my own situation, my daughter becoming a mother, and my son being arrested, I had a lot on my plate and no help.

My daughter wanted to get a job to take of her own baby and she did just that. It helped, but I felt I was responsible for everybody.

Chapter Seven

A Dark Place

I was struggling and going through a difficult time in my life. I needed financial help and I felt lonely. I ended up meeting this guy. I wanted a man in my life and thought that I needed a man. I was trying to fill that void. But the relationship was toxic. He was drinking alcohol; we was always fighting.

Nevertheless, I dealt with it because I needed help. I wasn't in a relationship for love, I knew what I needed; I needed help, and I felt lonely at times. A single mother taking care of kids by herself, it's a lot on her plate. Women in that situation sometimes don't know what to do. I was running out of options. I was still trying to make ends meet and thought that a man would help bring some stability into our lives. I was wrong.

That relationship made me extremely unhappy, and I stayed angry. My first mistake was moving too fast. I met this guy within two to three months and was in a relationship with this guy. So I basically introduced a stranger to my kids. My kids never knew why I moved a man in so quickly. But the truth is, I needed the man to take off some of the burden that I had on me. I needed help with my bills. I depended on his man to pay the bills. I depended on his man the entire time that we were together. Because I knew that he was going to pay to take care of things, I thought that he was the solution to all of my problems. But he became a bigger problem for me.

When he moved in, he was verbally abusive and an alcoholic. My kids fought with him and his behavior was terrible. He used to get drunk and drive, getting arrested, yelling, and arguing in public. I felt bad when my kids asked me, "Why did you move that man in here, who is he?" They had seen me do that a couple of times. I never told my kids that's what I did before. But I felt that was my reason for being in a relationship. I would get so stressed, so moving a man in to provide for us was the only thing going through my head whether the kids accepted it or not.

I thought that he was the first one who wanted to provide for me and my kids. Well, that took a toll on me, and I got so tired. It became so overwhelming. I went through this for two years and the relationship got worse and worse. I learned a lot from that relationship. I now know that you don't have to have a man in your life to make you happy. I thought that I couldn't deal with my financial situation, but the reality is that I had dealt with this situation, with my kids alone, without help, I could have done it without him.

But I felt I'd been doing it for too long; I was just so overwhelmed doing it, and I needed some relief.

Things were pretty difficult in trying to take care of six people and myself plus bills. I even went to jail for a ticket. The judge sentenced me to 30 days in jail. I had never been to jail, and I didn't know what my kids were doing on the outside. I was hurt and relied on my daughter to help me with the home until I got back. It was so hard being away from my kids.

I didn't know what to do at this time. I was trying to figure out why I was locked up. *Why did the judge put me here? Why can't I be home with my kids?* And each day, you know, I cried those 30 days because I'd never in my life, went to jail before. This was my first time being in jail and being gone from my kids and for 30 days. At that time, my oldest daughter, took care of everything. Whatever I left out there for her to pay, she did it for me. She was pretty much looking after my kids and her child, making sure everything was okay. I had a young son too, so she made sure that he went to school, made sure we were caught up on bills.

After I did my 30 days, and I came home, I was still with the guy, the arguments never stopped. And I just decided one day that I was tired, I wanted out. I told him that I no longer wanted to be with him again. The relationship was toxic, and I was just tired of it. I did two years of it, and I was done. Shortly after, we separated.

I began my fitness journey soon after. I was overweight and wanted to take care of my health. I felt I was not healthy mentally. I started my fitness journey because I wanted a better version of myself to evolve. I started taking my health seriously. I started to exercise. I started going to the gym. I motivated myself to work out before I started going to the gym. I began working out at home first, trying new foods, eating healthy, and making healthy choices. I started to have peace of mind. I noticed that I had fewer distractions, I could get focused and thought better and clearer. I became more motivated because the people around me were motivating me.

CHAPTER EIGHT

Discovering Me

I began self-love. I had to begin to love myself, I'd look in the mirror and tell myself, "I love you." I used to think I wasn't beautiful because at first, I didn't have on a lot of weight . Even though I was beautiful, the excess weight had me thinking that wasn't good enough. I met some fitness friends and started making better decisions. Me and my friends always worked out five days a week. I met a lot of fitness people and I'm still friends with them to this day. I met so many people and I enjoyed, walking, being fit, and meal prepping. I felt so good about myself. I really made a big change in my life just from working out. I'd never done something like that. I procrastinated for so many years.

I got to a point in my life where I was just really tired and wanted something different, something better. I had been saying that I wanted to do this, and it was the perfect time to do it without any distractions. I thought to myself, *I can really do this*. I began to feel good about myself and the clothes that I could wear and when I went shopping for clothes. Overall, I felt good, I looked good: self-love. I was around other people who were motivating and inspiring, which was a big impact on me. I began to inspire others. We were all working on our fitness journey.

November 23rd, I received a text message from my cousin saying that my grandma had passed away. So, I called her. It seemed unreal; I didn't want to believe it. I told my kids, and my kids were screaming and crying. Everybody was running through the house crying and I still didn't believe it. *It can't be true.*

I was just starting to feel good about myself; I was working out, my mindset was shifting, and grandma was telling me, I looked good, I looked nice. I used to talk to her about her health because she was a diabetic; I also tried to get my mom into fitness, but she would never take care of her health.

This can't be true. I don't believe that, kept going through my mind. I got dressed and told my kids to put on their clothes We drove over there and when we went into my grandmama's house, she was on the floor. She looked so beautiful and at peace. She was gone. She did her job and she's gone now. It's the only thing I can say. I knew that I was going to have my time to break down and cry, but not around everybody, in private. I was still in shock. I kept looking at her and thought, *"Why did you leave me?"* I started reminiscing about all the things my grandma did for me. If it weren't for my grandma, I don't know how far I would have gotten in my life. She saved me, even though she didn't do, and I was disappointed. But at the end of the day, she was there, she was like my mama. She was my mama when I didn't have a mama. I was torn.

She was all that I had. I kept asking myself, *What I'm going to do now? She died.* The things that I do know, she taught me. Grandma taught me everything that I know. She taught me how to read, write, AND SACRIFICE, the things that I'd need to know in life. When she passed, I felt a piece of me left with her.

I think that was the most difficult thing that I had ever dealt with because it put me in a depressive state. I wasn't eating, but I was trying to stay focused and working out. Many times while I working out, I'd break down, but I kept going although my focus wasn't really there. Every time I worked out, I kept going because of her, I didn't give up. My depression lasted about seven months.

That part of my life right there, I was still suffering. I still have my little my moments when I think about her, that night still plays in my head. I wish that she was here to see me write this book. I never told her that I wanted to write a book, I had it in my head years ago, but I never shared that with her.

I feel a little selfish and guilty sometimes because I felt like the black sheep in my family. I didn't call, or text my grandma or visit her. I wonder if anyone would ever apologize to me, did she know how I felt, was anyone going to address what had happened in my life? I always had high expectations, but they left me disappointed, and I'd feel let down.

I got really selfish and didn't want to talk to her. She would call and call. Maybe she was trying to see me. I never knew that she was sick because I never answered the phone. I didn't go around my grandma for maybe a year. I would stay away and was living my life and doing what I needed to do for my family. I kept ignoring her. When she died, I went back into my phone and saw that she had just called me and texted me days before she died. And I was just too selfish to respond to my grandma because of my feelings. That's just how I felt at the time and now I felt guilty. *Why didn't I pick up the phone, why didn't I go around my grandma.* That guilt ate me up inside for a long time.

It took her passing away for me to really start forgiving people. I took my grandma for granted. I knew that I can't keep holding grudges. I felt safe with her, and I was angry when she asked me to move. *She didn't come and save me. She's sent me off somewhere. Why did I have to go stay with somebody else?* I had to let that go. I learned a lot from her passing. I learned not to take things in life for granted, not to be too proud or selfish and to forgive others.

After my grandmama passed, I had a lot on my mind and because I was still on my fitness journey, I thought, *I want to come out with a fitness brand.*" The idea just came right off the top of my head. I told a friend and, she said, "Oh yeah."

I said, "Yes, I think I want to come out with a fitness brand." I told her the name: "She Fit." It was established in 2014 when I had the first thought, but not on paper, I didn't get my LLC until six years later. At this time, my youngest daughter got into some trouble, as she was hanging with the wrong crowd. She spent five months in the youth detention center. I was sad to be without my daughter. I would visit on weekends to make her feel better. I missed her so much; she was released on my birthday.

CHAPTER NINE

Losing Hope

I was engaged to a guy who was involved with another lady, but I was not aware of any of this. I began to see it as though it would get better, only to meet a man who was currently involved with another woman. Before we were engaged, me and this guy dated on and off for maybe a year. He then proposed to me, and I accepted his proposal. My kids were excited and happy. They began sharing it on social media because they were thinking that he was the one. I thought he was the one too. I had such strong feelings for this guy. I don't know much about the feeling that I had, but it felt good. I was shocked when he proposed to me.

We spent a lot of time together, I was really feeling this guy, I had a nice diamond ring too. And shortly after, this unknown person started to attack me on social media, telling me she was the girlfriend, that she'd been with him for a year. She went into the details about it. She texted me and kept attacking me through social media. At that time I was trying to ignore it because I was the one who got the ring, so I didn't care. I heard what she was saying but he proposed to me.

Every time I turned around, the lady kept appearing. I guess he was telling me one thing and was still seeing that lady. He was living a double life and I got caught in the middle of it. I was hurt. It hurt me so bad. I felt used, misled, and lied to. I thought, *Was this real?*" I started questioning myself, *How did I let you do this? How did you come into my life and mislead me? This, can you explain it? Why did you do this? How could you do this?*

My kids really liked him. I introduced him to my family and thought that he was different from the rest. He showed me different in the beginning, but no reason to not trust him. I didn't see any girlfriend. I was shown how you are supposed to treat a lady. Maybe he eventually revealed himself because he was doing so much to make me feel special. Or maybe that wasn't the real him. The relationship was toxic, and I didn't realize it because he was lying to me; I just didn't want to believe it. The situation took me to the point where I hated men and I didn't want trust them anymore.

And I didn't. I don't believe anything that a man says. I look back on that relationship and it was an eye-opener. I had never been engaged or married before. No one had ever given me a ring and I never had feelings like that for anyone. But it ended up not being what I had expected.

Knowing that he was engaged to me but had another girlfriend outside of the relationship, broke my heart. I was let down once again in life. That relationship didn't end on good terms. I felt deceived, hurt, heartbroken, and not good enough. I thought he would be the love of my life, but things got worse.. my youngest daughter was admitted in the hospital; she had gone portal blind in both eyes. The worse thing I experienced in life.. she recovered. At this point, I felt like I was losing everything; this was the roughest time in my life.

During all of this, I received a phone call from the hospital emergency room. I was told that my son had been shot four times and they didn't know if he was going to survive.

Everything in me shattered. I was shocked, scared, crying, and was trying to get to the hospital. This was the most devastating call I'd ever received. I later rushed to the hospital where my son was in critical care. After he was released from the hospital, I cared for him until he recovered.

All of this was happening while I was going through a moving situation. I was going through a difficult time. Times were rough. I went through it all, and I knew I had a purpose in life and a plan to become an entrepreneur and an author because I've always wanted to share my story. I live with scars and pain my entire life that I had hidden from the world, I was my own enemy. Standing in my own way of fear, finding my purpose.

CHAPTER TEN

Overcoming Fear

I had to overcome my fears and move out of my way. I lived in fear for a long time: fear of nothing is going to go well, all types of negative thoughts in my head, but I had goals and had to move away from that negativity. I had always wanted to start a business and write a book, and that was what I was determined to do.

I had always talked about writing this book for nearly four years and I would always ask myself, "Where am I going to get the money to do that and to start my business?" There was always a financial drawback and obstacle to get this completed. I said, "Let me go ahead and start a small business. First, I'll apply for my LLC and come up with the name, "She Fit." I already had the name, *She Fit,* but didn't have an LLC. I started to sell my fitness apparel brand, still I had some fear because I had never been an entrepreneur. I didn't know the ins and outs of a business.

Regardless of my fears, I kept pushing myself. Sometimes thoughts would creep in: *Maybe this isn't meant for me to do this, or should I do this?* I was still going back and forth trying to convince myself, but I knew that I wanted to do this. I knew that I wanted to write my book but was living in fear. The fear caused me to procrastinate and doubt myself a lot. It had me in a mental prison, ashamed of people knowing my story. It was difficult to move forward because people would know my truth. I wanted to tell people my story but the shame that I felt was overtaking me at times. I would sometimes share my story with others, but I used to leave things out because I was embarrassed and ashamed. However, I soon realized that it was truly fear that I needed to overcome. Once I did that, there was no turning back. I was determined to live my life without any fear.

I started my business and was gaining customers. I started to receive reviews and my customers loved the quality of the clothing. It makes me so happy to know that others are happy, when I hear good feedback; it makes me feel good.

My success made me overexcited to finally complete one goal. I wanted to write my book next. I was all in. I started eating healthy even more because I had to represent my brand, especially because I was selling fitness clothing; I want to inspire my customers. I want to inspire others. That's what made me come up with the brand, my fitness journey, wanting to inspire others and to have fitness-inspired outfits. I love to inspire people. I love to share my story, especially my fitness journey.

It's been two years that I have not eaten any meat. That right there meant a lot to me. It means a lot to have reached my goals and to watch my customers accomplish their goals also and that they feel good in their clothes. Their reviews played a big factor in my business. Everything was going so well, then all of a sudden, it all went left. For some reason, I couldn't get my website up and running and people that I trusted were not giving me what I was paying for.

So when I didn't get the website done, doubt started to come back. I thought, *It's not meant for me*, all the negative stuff was coming into my head again. I thought about it. I slept on it and said, "No, I'm not going to do this. I'm going to move forward with it. And I'm going to do it. I'll open up my Instagram page and that's how I'm going to do it." And that's what I did. I proceeded, I didn't let the website stop me. I kept going. I kept moving. I kept pushing. Shortly after that, my page got removed, I thought, *What happened?* Three or four days passed, and I created another page. I got an email from social media saying that someone reported my page due to my business name. I didn't know what they meant about the business name or what that could be about? Instagram told me that it was a confrontation . They told me that somebody else used that business name on Instagram and all other platforms. I was then told to never use that name. I never knew anyone had ever used that name; I didn't steal their name.

I got very discouraged and disappointed because I didn't have a website, I feared losing all of my customers. *Why is this happening to me? This was my goal. why all it is just coming down on* me. *I'm doing what's right.* I just kept questioning myself. When my page was removed, I was very disappointed, but I kept pushing.

I kept moving on. I had to figure it out. I always had to figure things out in my life; this was nothing new. I had gotten over everything else that had come my way that was meant to destroy me. I always get through it. Shortly after my page was removed, I received another email, and it was from a lawyer. The lawyer was telling me they were sending me the trademark paperwork from the other business and to not use, "She Fit" anymore. I was going back and forth. I told her that I came up with name years ago. I'm not giving it up. I stood on that. That's my brand. My logo is on my brand. And she showed me their paperwork. "No, my client had her paperwork first from 2014," the lawyer said. I thought, *In 2014, I didn't know anything about an LLC.* No one ever taught me about the business side of things. Therefore, I never thought about it. And I kept going back and forth with the lawyer.

I said, "Okay, what if I take this out?" And she killed every idea that I sent her.

 She kept sending me, "You have to take the She Fit out or else we will sue you."

The disappointment was all over me. I felt so discouraged as I was looking at all my inventory. I had so many products with my name branded on them. I thought, *This was mine.* As I lay in bed and started to think about all the things that I went through and how everything that I had gone through in my life, I overcame. I realized that I was fearless. I am that woman. I don't give up. I've lived through a lot of things in life, saw a lot of things, and have been in a lot of situations, I'm fearless. *I'm not giving up, this is who I am. This is my name, it comes from me. I'm not feeling any fear anymore.* That's how the name, "Fearless Woman," came about.

CHAPTER ELEVEN

Fearless Woman

There were so many lessons that I learned throughout my life. I learned to walk my own path. Good things, don't come easy. Never fail to try one more time. Make every moment count. Every action has a reaction. Even when you're feeling unprepared, there is a chance of accomplishing your goals. Meeting people that had burned me in the past helped me to learn things because of this; I believed in myself and overcame fears. I kept going and you can too. I didn't give up. Giving up wasn't an option for me. What I believed in, is what I became. I'm brave, strong, determined, resilient, and unstoppable. I'm not willing to let anything stop me. Turning my pain into power, I was determined to figure out whatever I needed to do, on my own. As I went into business, when I didn't know something, I basically found everything on my own. My publisher for my book, I found you on Instagram because I was determined to write a book. I had to find my own publisher and my own vendors. I did everything on my own, even marketing my business, I did everything, no one ever taught me that.

Learning everything on my own taught me a lesson. I know how to apply myself. I know what to do now and what to avoid. The things that I do know to do, a year ago, I didn't know. I know now that I can't keep an idea in my head, I have to put it on paper to show others that it's mine.

I stayed positive and didn't give up options. I got discouraged but kept going. I didn't let go of the possibilities that I could succeed. I figured it out. I knew I was going to figure something out, I encouraged my own self. I remember sitting back, trying to figure out how I was going to overcome situations. There was always a way out of every situation.

At this point in my life, I can truly say that I love myself. I don't look for love anymore. I don't need to look for love. I've made peace within myself. I love myself for making better decisions. I'm no longer depending on a man's love. I don't need a man to complete me. I don't feel that missing void anymore or crave for a man. I'm a totally different person now. I'm still a work in progress, but I have come a long way. I learned to accept the fact that I'm single and have no distractions right now. I overcame mental and physical abuse, childhood trauma that I suffered throughout my life.

My past is not my prison, I have overcome everything. I'm proud of myself for writing my first book and rebranding (Fearless Woman Collection). My mindset has changed. All the negative thoughts have become positive thoughts. My thoughts became my reality, by thinking positively and not allowing doubt and fear to overcome me. I see life differently. I see my vision clearly and it's taking me places. I found peace. I now see the bigger picture. Finally, I have brought the vision to life. I'm proud of myself for becoming the woman that I am today. Having a closer relationship with my mother. I'm so proud of my mother for getting clean and sober. My kids became business owners: a proud mother. I feel FREE, living my truth. Now I know all the pain I've gone through was preparing me for something bigger: finding my purpose.

CHAPTER TWELVE

New Beginning

M y mind is different from years ago and even a year ago. I'm not thinking negative thoughts anymore, I'm not doubting myself, I'm more positive. I'm speaking more positively. I'm telling myself I can do it, I will do it. I'm going to do it. My mindset is totally different from times when I used to always think of fear and doubting myself. I had those in my mind at first, but my mindset has totally changed my life. I believe more in myself now. I'm there mentally; I'm more focused now. I'm more determined. This part of my life is the new beginning. I overcame the things that were meant to destroy me.

Having peace is so important to me right now. I have peace and I love my peace and it feels good where I'm at now. I don't have any distractions. It's completely different from when I first started my business. My new business name truly reflects me as a whole, my life entirely. This brand is more of me. It's the meaning behind the brand that I'm proud of. It took for me to go through all of that, to get here, but I'm here. Everything happened in time. I believe in myself more. I see the bigger picture now. I see myself going somewhere. I see myself going places. I see myself on book tours and at speaking events. I'm envisioning all of that and it's going to happen because I believe in myself. I don't have those negative thoughts in my mind anymore. I just want my story to help a lot of women out there who are going through it or have been through it. I was once that woman. So that was my reason for sharing my stories, to help others out there. I want to help people to overcome the same things that I overcame. From having a mom with a drug addiction, abuse being a teen mom, losing my kids to the system, to becoming a business owner, entrepreneur, and an author. I never imagined doing all of the things that I'm doing, but I had hope and here I am, you're reading my book. I'm extremely proud of myself.

My mom and I have a better relationship. We talk a lot, laugh, and I help her with certain things. We talk on the phone every day. I know things are not going to happen overnight, but I want a much better relationship with my mom. Building a healthy relationship with mom is important to me. I'm learning more about her and she's learning more about me. Mom is now sharing the things with me that help me to understand everything better. I love my mom, always. She wasn't a bad mother and my mom got caught up in some things, and a lot of other women did in those times.

I still struggle with the things that have happened and I have negative feelings about them. I don't blame my mom, she couldn't help that she was sick. I look at the present moment and not the past. I have a great relationship with my kids. I'm just excited to see where everybody's going. We came a long way. We had to from struggle and had tough times, but we made it out. We didn't have a good life growing up, it wasn't perfect, but I'm just excited to see where life's going to take us. I'm here to support everybody and I've decided to start this new chapter of my life. I'm totally FREE!

ABOUT AUTHOR

My name is **Chana Brown,** and I live in Atlanta GA. I'm a mother of five children, an entrepreneur and the author of "Fearless Woman." Becoming an entrepreneur and author was my vision. Inspiring others is my passion. I decided to share my story to the world: how I overcame every obstacle in my life. Finding my purpose, bringing my story to life to encourage women to believe in themselves, and not to give up. Anything is possible. Be unstoppable. Be Fearless.

Made in United States
North Haven, CT
10 November 2021